CW00429247

Pirate Ships

Alison Hawes

RIGBY

Contents

Pirate ships

Pirates travelled by water. They used many different kinds of ship or boat. Most pirates liked to travel in small ships and boats. But some pirates used large war ships.

Small ships and boats made good pirate ships. They could move quickly and were easy to steer.

Small pirate ships could also hide from bigger ships!

5

A small pirate ship had room for about 75 pirates. It would have one or two masts. It had up to fourteen cannons.

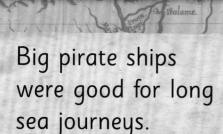

Big pirate ships were good for long sea journeys.

Big pirate ships were heavy and slow. But they had room for up to 200 pirates on board! These ships had more sails and more cannons too.

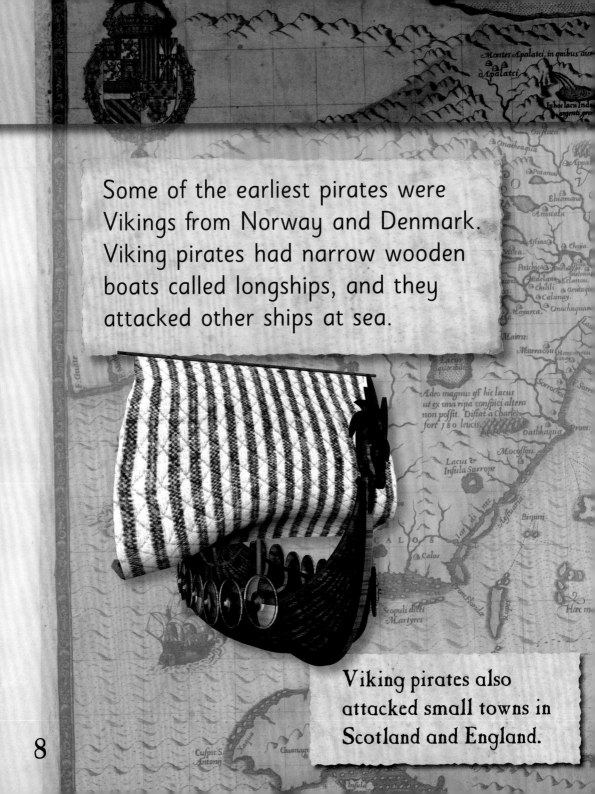

Some of the earliest pirates were Vikings from Norway and Denmark. Viking pirates had narrow wooden boats called longships, and they attacked other ships at sea.

Viking pirates also attacked small towns in Scotland and England.

Longships had oars and a sail.
They could travel fast in the sea or
up rivers, and they could land almost
anywhere.

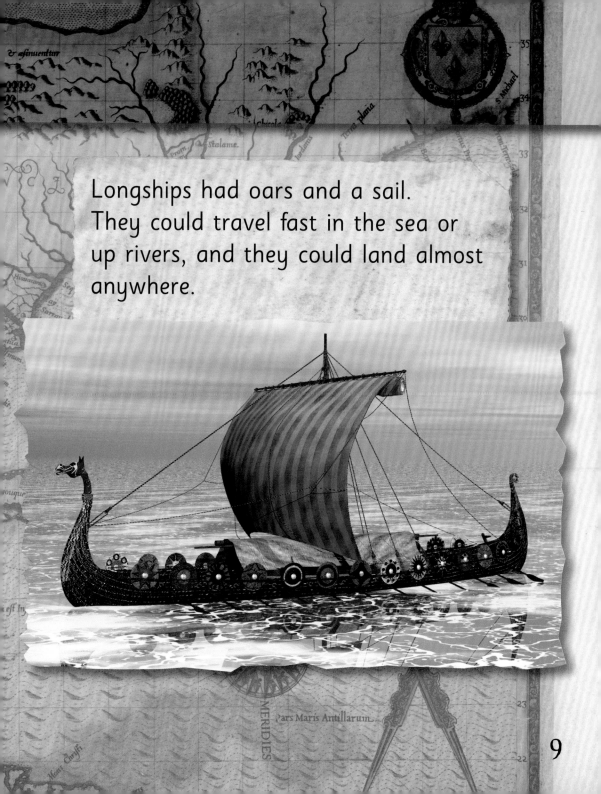

Working on a pirate ship

Pirates did lots of different jobs on a pirate ship.

One **sailor** stood in the **lookout**. He looked out for ships and land.

The **carpenter** looked after the wooden parts of the ship, like the **mast**.

The **gunner** looked after the guns and **cannon**.

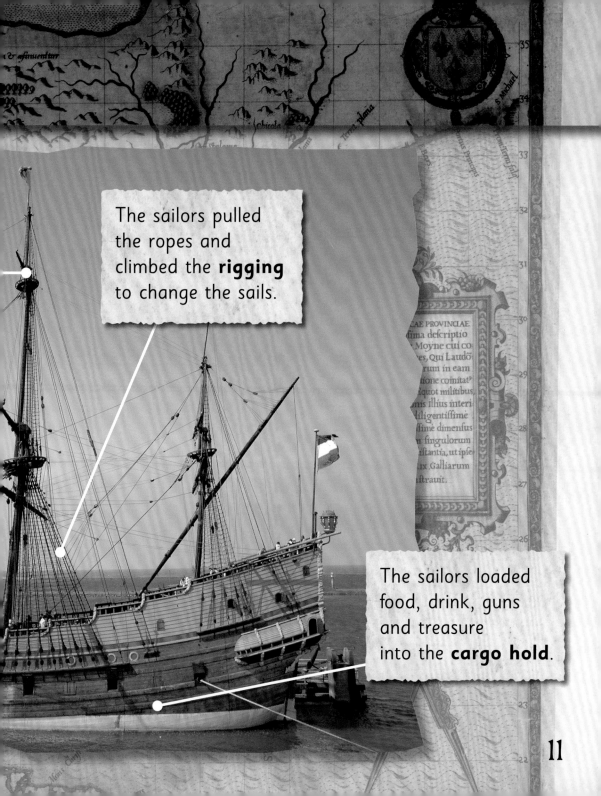

The sailors pulled the ropes and climbed the **rigging** to change the sails.

The sailors loaded food, drink, guns and treasure into the **cargo hold**.

11

The **Captain** was the chief pirate. He was in charge of everyone on the ship. He decided which ships to rob and he shared out the treasure.

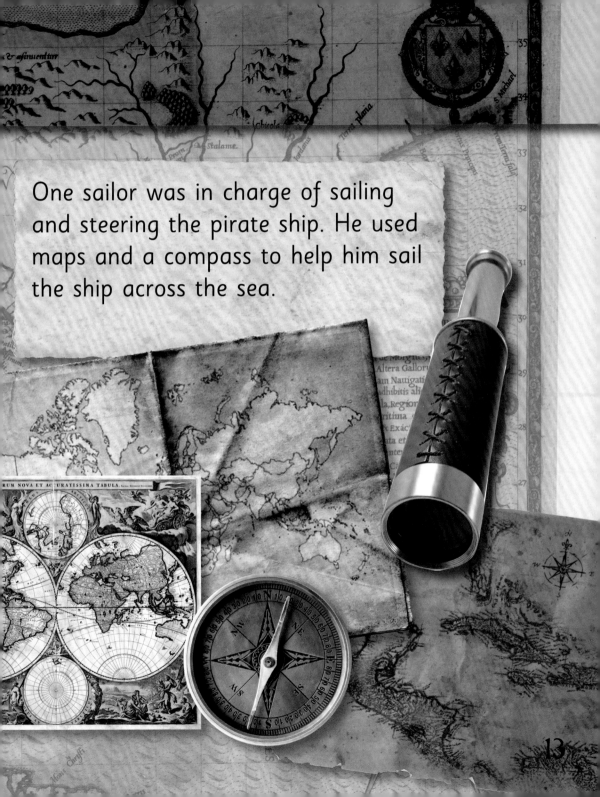

One sailor was in charge of sailing and steering the pirate ship. He used maps and a compass to help him sail the ship across the sea.

One sailor looked after the rigging and the anchor on a pirate ship. He told the sailors how to fix the sails so that the ship sailed at the right speed.

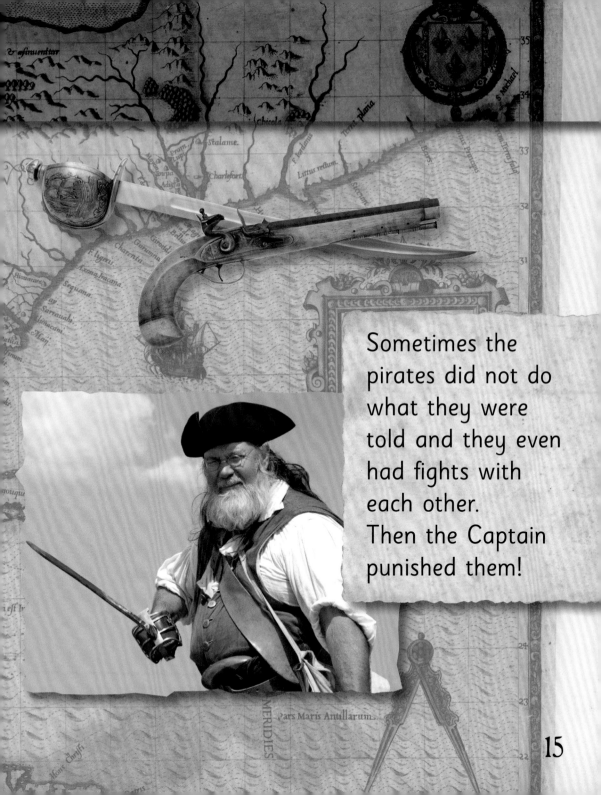

Sometimes the pirates did not do what they were told and they even had fights with each other.
Then the Captain punished them!

Galleons

Pirates often attacked galleons. Galleons were large sailing ships, and they carried expensive goods from one country to another.

Galleons often carried gold and silver.

Galleons were strong, wooden ships. But they were heavy and slow. Pirate ships were faster than galleons. They could easily catch up with a galleon.

Pirate ships had to take care!
A galleon often had more guns and
cannons than a pirate ship.

Galleons had up to 60 cannons
and 200 men on board.

Sometimes lots of galleons sailed across the sea together. Sometimes 100 galleons sailed together! They travelled together to stop the pirates attacking them. But this didn't always work!

Modern pirates

Modern pirates travel by water. They rob people at sea and on land. They use different kinds of boat. But most modern pirates like to use small fast boats.

Modern pirates often use speedboats because they are light and easy to steer. They have large motors that make the boats travel very fast when the police chase them.

Pirates today attack many different kinds of ship. Sometimes, they attack big cruise ships. Sometimes they attack small fishing boats.

Sometimes, modern pirates attack ships carrying expensive goods. They may even attack large tankers carrying oil!

Index